Washington's Historical Courthouses

Ray Graves

ELFIN COVE PRESS
1481 130th Avenue NE
Bellevue, WA 98005

"WASHINGTON'S HISTORICAL COURTHOUSES"

copyright © 2002 by RAY GRAVES

ISBN#0-944958-26-5
LOC#2002 141510

© Eric Erickson--Photographer, unless otherwise noted
Bernie Kuntz--Project Manager
Lisa McCoy--Editor
C Wilson Trull--Text and cover design

Printed in Korea

1 3 5 7 9 10 8 6 4 2

TABLE OF CONTENTS

3

P r e f a c e

In a legal career spanning nearly 50 years, I have had the opportunity to appear in nearly half of Washington's 39 county courthouses. During this time, some of the courthouses have been torn down and replaced with new buildings. Those destroyed during my legal career were the Pierce, Yakima, Whitman, Whatcom, and Kittitas County courthouses. Only the outstanding efforts of dedicated county officials, local historical societies, and community volunteers have saved and restored other courthouses.

Some of our historical courthouses have suffered severe damage from natural events; for example, the Grays Harbor Courthouse at Montesano was damaged by earthquake; and others have succumbed to natural elements, with time alone causing some deterioration. While some counties have found the needed resources to restore their courthouses, others have not, thus stressing the need of the state legislature to assist local governments in maintaining and restoring these historical buildings.

As I traveled about the state and made court appearances in a large number of these courthouses, I came to realize what an important part of Washington's architectural history they are. As a result, I was determined to put together some of that history with photographs of those historical courthouses.

While history has no cut-off point and is, of course, ongoing, I decided to include photographs of those courthouses built in 1930 or before and still in active use. For those courthouses that were constructed after 1930, I have included photographs of those that were replaced. Although I have included some history of county formation, selection of the county seat, and a bit about the architects, this book is really meant to provide a pictorial review of the courthouses.

A book of this type is naturally dependent on the photography, and for that, we have to thank the talented Erick Erickson, whose home and studio are at Cathlamet, Washington, on the banks of the Columbia River.

Although a great deal of my own research has gone into the making of this book, it could not have been completed without the enthusiastic help of county employees and the employees and volunteers of the many historical societies. I have had help from more than 100 of those people, and will not attempt to name them here.

I must also thank my wife, Joan, who not only read and commented on the material I wrote, but also encouraged me on to conclusion. My daughter, Valerie, the computer expert, helped me with formatting my computer for special tasks. My son, Jon, the architect, was an invaluable source of information about the architecture.

I n t r o d u c t i o n   b y

Gerry L. Alexander

Chief Justice of the

Washington State Supreme Court

Anyone who loves the law or historic buildings or both will be delighted to leaf their way through Ray Graves' excellent work, *Washington's Historical Courthouses*. Although pictures of courthouses from each of our 39 counties is displayed, unlike other books that are devoted to depicting the courthouses of this state, Mr. Graves' book does not, in every instance, display a picture of a county's current courthouse. Instead, he has chosen to feature a county's most historically significant courthouse.

Fortunately, many of Washington's old courthouse buildings have survived, and most of them are still serving as the county courthouse. This is somewhat amazing since earthquakes, burgeoning populations, urban renewal, and other forces have conspired over the years to bring about the destruction of some of Washington's truly significant buildings, including, sadly, some of our great courthouses. Many of those long-gone courthouses are pictured in Ray Graves' book together with others that still exist.

Seeing pictures of some of the beautiful courthouse buildings that did not escape the wrecker's ball makes one wish that we could turn back the hands of time in order to rescue those buildings. It also makes one appreciate the efforts of county officials, local historians, and ordinary citizens in many of our counties who successfully fought to retain their courthouses.

Like Ray Graves, I appeared in many of Washington's historic courthouses during my days as a lawyer. In addition, during my almost 30 years as a judge and justice, I have had the unique opportunity to preside over trials and hearings or participate in ceremonies in more than half of our state's existing courthouses. In my travels as a lawyer or judge to those courthouses, I have invariably been struck by the magnificence of many of those buildings, as well as by the significance such buildings have had to the life of the communities in which they are located. One only need visit county seats like Port Townsend, Dayton, Spokane, South Bend, and Montesano, places where a beautiful and historic courthouse still dominates the skyline, to know what I am talking about. Each of these buildings and more are depicted in Ray Graves' book together with informative material about how and when each of our counties was formed and a description of how the site of the county seat was determined. In addition, Mr. Graves provides interesting information about the architects and contractors who were instrumental in erecting these buildings. This book, in short, is a treasure trove of information about the unique buildings that have served or still serve as the seat of justice in each of our counties.

One might ask—is it important to know about our county courthouses? I answer that question with an emphatic yes. Our nation, after all, prides itself on being a nation of laws and not of men, and there is no greater symbol of our devotion to the rule of law than the county courthouse. Thank heaven there is a courthouse in every county of every state in the Union and that it is the place where men and women have labored and will continue to labor in the eternal quest to provide equal and perfect justice to all.

Washington is fortunate to have some beautiful courthouses that have survived the ravages of time. Unfortunately, a few great ones have gotten away. However, thanks to Ray Graves' devotion to a subject that he clearly loves, we can enjoy viewing the best the past and present have to offer us.

Establishing the County Seats

The choice of locations for Washington's county seats is a part of the state's more colorful history. The ultimate decisions were made, in most cases, by a vote of the county's citizens or by the legislature and, in one instance, by the U.S. Congress.

The fight for county seats demonstrated how economically important that designation was to the town or city chosen. In earlier times, the county seats were even more the center of the county's activities than they are today. The fights also illustrated how much a part of the western frontier we were. Some of the more interesting struggles are described in this chapter.

One of the early fights for county seat location was in Pacific County in 1893. Oysterville had been the county seat until the 1892 election, when the voters chose South Bend. When the county records were not forthcoming, some citizens of South Bend "kidnapped" those records and took them by boat to South Bend. A similar kidnapping is reported to have taken place to enable Mount Vernon to remove the Skagit County records from La Conner.

In Skamania County, where the county seat had been established at Lower Cascades (now Bonneville), a group of "rowdies" raided the courthouse in 1893 and took all the county records to Stevenson. Although court action was threatened, it never took place, and Stevenson remains the county seat today.

In Cowlitz County, numerous elections were held between 1872, when Kalama was established as the county seat, and 1922, when it was finally moved to Kelso. Newspaper cartoons in the 1906 election campaign showed the prominent citizens bribing the voters with promises of money and property.

In 1890, after a hotly contested election in Clallam County, Port Angeles won the county seat away from

Dungeness. Fearing trouble, 25 men from Port Angeles went to Dungeness on horseback, carrying guns. They took along wagons to bring back the records, and when no fight ensued, they returned with the records.

In Kitsap County, from 1864 to 1892, the town of Teekalet was twice voted the county seat, but the officials refused to give up the records both times, and they remained in Port Madison until 1891. In an election held that year, they were finally moved to Sydney (Port Orchard).

In Snohomish County, legal battles ended up in the Washington State Supreme Court on three occasions before the county seat was finally moved from Snohomish City to Everett.

In 1884, it took the United States Congress to settle the bitter dispute in Garfield County between Pomeroy and Pataka City. Pomeroy won out.

Perhaps the most notorious contest took place in Lincoln County in 1884. Sprague received the most votes, but the number of votes it received exceeded the total voting population of the county! Davenport claimed the names of the Sprague voters were taken from tombstones and train passengers going through the area. Although Davenport sought court relief, it also called for help from the nearby settlers, who came armed with Winchesters, shotguns, and six-shooter guns to keep the records in Davenport. Sprague then formed a posse led by its sheriff-elect, John Cody. When the posse arrived in Davenport, they were confronted by one A. W. Hutchinson, who, with his long-barreled revolver, offered to shoot it out with the sheriff, with the county seat going to the town of the survivor! Fortunately, cooler heads prevailed, and the records were finally surrendered to Sprague.

About the Architecture and Architects

This book is not intended to provide a detailed analysis of courthouse architecture, but rather a pictorial review of Washington's courthouses. However, some general information about the various forms of architecture to be found among the courthouses should be helpful to the reader in looking at the photography and the actual courthouses. At the end of this book is a glossary of the architectural and building terms used here.

Information about the architects who designed the 39 courthouses pictured in this book is not readily accessible. Nevertheless, some information is available and tells us something of why the architectural styles resulted. The courthouses have usually been located in the heart of the county seat and frequently on a site commanding a good view of the city.

The architectural style of the courthouses varies widely. In most instances, the characterization of the architectural style in each courthouse pictured in this book was the choice of someone other than the author, and in some cases, there is no agreement as to what that style is. Undoubtedly, any disparity arises in part because most of the courthouses are not the result of a "pure" architectural design, but rather reflect several influences. An exaggerated example of this is the Columbia County Courthouse, which has been described as having a building of Italianate design with a Queen Anne cupola.

Architectural designs for the courthouses range from Romanesque (Jefferson County) to Italianate (Columbia County). Among the other styles, we find California, or Spanish, Mission (Snohomish, Douglas, and Okanogan counties), Classical Revival or Neo-Classic (Pacific, Grant, and Franklin counties) and Beaux Arts-Roman Revival and Palladian Beaux Arts (Grays Harbor and Chelan counties). And Art Deco (Thurston and Mason Counties).

10

The most prolific of the courthouse designers was Willis A. Ritchie (1864-1931). Ritchie was born in Ohio and studied architecture through a correspondence course. He opened his first office in Lima, Ohio, but two years later moved to Winfield, Kansas, where a building boom was taking place. In 1889, after the great fire in Seattle, Ritchie, at age 25, moved there to take advantage of the rebuilding. The first courthouse he designed was the King County Courthouse on "Profanity Hill" (1889-1891). At the same time, he designed the Whatcom County Courthouse in Bellingham (1889-1891). His next two courthouses were the Jefferson County Courthouse at Port Townsend (1890-1892) and the Thurston County Courthouse in Olympia (1890-1892). Both are still in use, although the Thurston County building is no longer used as a courthouse. The Jefferson County Courthouse was the largest of those designed by Ritchie in Western Washington. Following those, Ritchie designed the Clark County Courthouse in Vancouver (1891-1892). His final courthouse design was in Spokane (1893-1896), which is still in use today. It is perhaps the grandest of them all, and is said to be designed in the Chateau style and modeled after two famous chateaus in the Loire Valley of France. During the construction of this courthouse, Ritchie moved to Spokane, where he ended his career.

It appears that Ritchie was influenced in his design by the great American architect H. H. Richardson. Ritchie's designs were all in a grand style, ranging from the Chateauesque style of Spokane's courthouse to the Romanesque style of Port Townsend's. However, as one writer has observed, the interiors of these large public buildings rarely live up to expectations created by the exteriors. Those interiors are rather ordinary and sometimes drab. Still, there are many courthouses with interesting interiors, an outstanding example being the Grays Harbor County Courthouse.

It is noteworthy that in the same period in which Ritchie was designing courthouses in Washington, architects Proctor and Dennis designed the Pierce County Courthouse (1892), which was patterned after the courthouse in Pittsburgh, Pennsylvania, designed by H. H. Richardson. This style is sometimes referred to as Richardsonian Romanesque.

There was a brief period when the California Mission style of architecture became popular in the Northwest. The first of these was designed by Seattle architect August F. Heide in 1911, and was built for Snohomish County in Everett. It is thought that Heide was influenced by the architectural theme of the Centennial Exposition in Portland, Oregon, in 1905. It was there that Heide had designed the Washington State Building for the Fair. That building was near the European Exhibits Building, which featured the Mission style. Heide had also designed the previous Snohomish County Courthouse, but in a Chateauesque style.

In 1914, architect George H. Keith of Spokane designed the Okanogan County Courthouse in the Mission, or Spanish, Colonial Revival style. During the period in which the Snohomish and Okanogan Courthouses were designed and constructed, numerous other buildings in the state were designed and constructed in the same or similar Mission style.

Two courthouses designed and constructed in the Neo-Classic or Classical Revival style were those in Pacific County (1910) and Franklin County (1912). These two courthouses were designed by architect C. Lewis Wilson, first of Chehalis and later of Seattle. Both courthouses feature well-decorated art glass interior domes and more elaborate interiors than was normal at the time. At the end of this book is a list of the architects who designed Washington's surviving courthouses (see the Appendix). Other than Ritchie and Wilson, only three other architects designed more than one of these courthouses, one of whom was George H. Keith, who, in addition to the Okanogan Courthouse, also designed the Grant County Courthouse.

Joseph H. Wohleb of Olympia designed both the Thurston County Courthouse (across from the state capitol grounds) and the Mason County Courthouse.

Newton C. Gaunt, a Portland, Oregon, architect, designed both the Douglas and Wahkiakum County Courthouses, as well as the old Yakima County Courthouse, now destroyed but pictured in this book.

The Counties

The 1914 Adams County Courthouse, courtesy of the Ritzville Public Library, from the Kendrick Collection.

A d a m s   C o u n t y

A dams County, along with Franklin County, was one of the last two counties to be carved out of what was once a larger Whitman County. This action took place in 1883 by action of the state legislature. Adams County was named after the second President of the United States, John Adams. Ritzville has always been the county seat, and the reason it was chosen was simple—there was no other town in the county at the time.

The first county courthouse was a wooden building constructed about 1884. A second courthouse was built in the late 1800s and it was replaced by a third courthouse in 1914. This courthouse remained in service until 1941, when a modern courthouse was built. The 1941 courthouse remains in service today. The 1914 courthouse is pictured here.

The 1899 Asotin County Courthouse, courtesy of the Asotin County Historical Society.

The Ayers Hotel, now the Asotin County Courthouse, courtesy of the Asotin County Court Historical Society.

Asotin County was created out of a portion of Garfield County in 1883. "Asotin" is a Native American word meaning "Eel Creek." The county seat has always been near the town of Asotin, which was originally an Indian village. Chief Looking Glass, the second-ranking chieftain of the Nez Perce Nation, had presided there.

In 1899, the first permanent courthouse was built. It was a two-story, 40-by-60-foot building constructed at a cost of $3,975. That courthouse remained in use until 1936, when it was completely destroyed by fire. During the following two years, various buildings were used as courthouses. In this period, an election was held as a result of pressure to move the county seat to Clarkston. The effort failed, and the county seat remained at Asotin.

In need of a permanent place for county operations, the county commissioners finally decided to use the Ayers Hotel as a courthouse. The county had foreclosed on the hotel for failure to pay taxes. Rumor had it that a brothel operated on the third floor, but in any event, the hotel was remodeled and remains as Asotin County's courthouse today. It is the only building in the state in use as a courthouse that was not originally constructed for that purpose.

A Superior Court judge "rides circuit" between Asotin, Columbia and Garfield counties, presiding in all three courts.

The present-day Benton County Courthouse (1927).

B e n t o n   C o u n t y

Benton County was carved out of portions of Yakima and Klickitat counties in 1905. The county is circled on three sides by the Columbia River. It was named after Thomas Hart Benton, a United States Senator from Missouri. While the county seat is in Prosser, where it has always been, most trials in Benton County are held in the counties Law and Justice center in Kennewick WA.

A series of temporary quarters was used, including two hotels, before the county finally constructed a new courthouse in 1927. The courthouse is faced in brick, with an elaborate front consisting of two columns and a balcony below the pediment. The interior of the courthouse has been completely remodeled.

Benton County Courtroom.

The courthouse was designed by architect George M. Rasque, of Link & Rasque, and constructed by Ernest White & Company of Twin Falls, Idaho, at a cost of $87,000, excluding the heating and plumbing, which cost an extra $8,275. In 1944 and 1946, additions were added to the rear of the building.

The courthouse was entered in the National Registry of Historic Places on December 12, 1976.

The present-day Chelan County Courthouse (1924).

Chelan County

Chelan County was formed from parts of Kittitas and Okanogan counties in 1899 10 years after Washington was made a state. The name "Chelan" is a Native American word referring to "waters," which in this instance probably referred to Lake Chelan. Upon the county's creation, Wenatchee became its county seat and remains so today.

The first courthouse was a three-story brick hotel, which was used by the county as the courthouse until 1924, when the new one was constructed. The old courthouse reverted back to a hotel until it was remodeled. Portions of it are recognizable today.

Like most counties, Chelan has had to construct new facilities to the rear of the existing courthouse to accommodate growth.

The present courthouse was constructed in 1924. The total cost of the building, including furniture, was approximately $400,000.

The architectural firm of Morrison, Stimson & Company of Spokane was awarded the contract to design and supervise the construction of the building. The architect in that firm who actually did the design and supervision was Ludwig Solberg. He later became a Wenatchee resident and was responsible for designing many of its well-known buildings. He also designed a later addition to the Okanogan County Courthouse.

An exterior light standard of Chelan's courthouse.

The Chelan County Courthouse is a four-story brick building sitting on a base of granite brought from Index, Washington. The building is trimmed with terra cotta designs, and the corridors are laid with Alaskan marble. The building design has been described by county officials as Palladian Beaux Arts. It was constructed by Jarl & Lasker, contractors from Great Falls, Montana. The front of the building features numerous carved and scrolled designs.

21

C l a l l a m   C o u n t y

Clallam County was created in 1854 when the territorial legislature carved it out of the northern portion of Jefferson County. The name "Clallam" is a Native American word meaning "strong people."

In 1860, the county seat was established near Dungeness (then New Dungeness) at a place known as "Whiskey Flat." The county seat remained there for 30 years. In 1890, after a contest between Port Crescent, Dungeness, and Port Angeles, the county seat was changed to Port Angeles. After relocation to Port Angeles, the county activities took place in numerous buildings until 1915, when the present courthouse was completed.

The courthouse was designed by architect Francis W. Grant of Seattle, Washington, in what has been characterized as Early American Design. The building was constructed by Sound Construction Company at a total cost of $57,688. The roofline of the building was changed in 1936 when dormer windows were added to make three small rooms for the engineers and drafting department.

The building has a clock tower 16 feet square with a four-sided clock and above it, a bell, both of which are electrically operated.

The clock itself has an interesting history. It was manufactured by the E. Howard Tower Clock Co. of Boston, Massachusetts, in 1880. This is the same company that provided the clock for Jefferson County at Port Townsend. The clock, along with the bell, was shipped around Cape Horn in South America to Seattle in 1885, but the purchaser never claimed them. They sat on the dock until architect Grant discovered and purchased them for the courthouse, where they were installed at a cost of $5,115.

The present-day Clallam County Courthouse (1915).

Stained glass over the central courthouse lobby.

Clallam County
(c o n t i n u e d)

The face of the clock is eight feet wide and is of frosted glass. The hands have only a forward motion, which causes a problem in changing to Daylight Savings Time and back again. The hands must be moved ahead in 30-minute increments to let the clock chime at each setting. It is wound automatically, and a cable from the striking mechanism goes up about 18 feet through the roof and is attached to the clapper (looks like a hammer), which strikes the outside of the bell. Originally, glass batteries ran the clock, but they have now been replaced by electricity.

The tower and walls of the building are of burlap brick with a tin roof and zinc finials. The dome of the tower is supported by both wood and metal columns. The cornices of the building are of galvanized iron. There are columns and windowsills of terra cotta. The original furnace in the building was fired by wood.

Inside the courthouse, the fine-looking marble substance is actually scagliola, or imitation marble. It is made from cement, plaster of paris, powdered alum, water, and fine sawdust tinted ochre, umber, or dark green with dark horse hair stretched out in the wet scagliola and left to dry. The scagliola was prepared and sawed to specification on-site. The skylight inside the courthouse was covered for many years because of leaks, but has now been cleaned, repaired, and artificial lighting installed over it.

This building was restored in 1999, as was the furniture and judge's bench in the original courtroom on the second floor. However some court proceedings are conducted in an adjacent building. Complete plans of the original building and furniture remain intact. The courthouse was registered with Washington State as historic property in 1971.

The marble-like interior—actually scagliola.

Clallam County Courtroom.

The 1892 Clark County Courthouse, courtesy of Washington State University Libraries, No. 78995.

C l a r k   C o u n t y

Clark County was originally created as the Vancouver District in 1844 as part of the Oregon Territory. In 1849, the name was changed to "Clark" in honor of Captain William Clark of the Lewis and Clark Expedition. The district was the first political unit organized in what is now Washington State.

Originally, the county stretched from the Pacific Ocean to the Rocky Mountains and included parts of Idaho and Montana. While still part of the Oregon Territory, the county seat was established at Vancouver, Washington.

In 1892, a third courthouse was constructed, the previous two having been destroyed by fire. The 1892 ornate courthouse depicted here was designed by architect Willis A. Ritchie of Seattle, who was to become the designer of six of Washington's county courthouses. Two of these are still in use today. They are the Jefferson County Courthouse at Port Townsend and the Spokane County Courthouse at Spokane. A third, the Thurston County Courthouse at Olympia, still stands, minus the original tower, but is no longer used as a courthouse. The others, including the one in Clark County, have all been razed.

It was the fear of fire that caused Clark County to construct a new, more modern courthouse in 1940.

The present-day Columbia County Courthouse (1887).

Columbia County

This county was created out of Walla Walla County in 1875 and originally contained the additional area now encompassed by both Garfield and Asotin counties. Dayton has always been its county seat. Its courthouse is the oldest in the state, having been built in 1887, two years before Washington became a state.

The cost of the courthouse construction was $38,069. While most counties have added additional facilities, usually to the rear of existing courthouses, Columbia's has proved adequate because its population has decreased.

The courthouse was designed by local architect William Burrows, who is said to have designed the courthouse at Pendleton, Oregon. The general contractor was the Gilbert H. Moen Company.

The courthouse was designed in the Italianate style, with the exception of a Greek cross on top 71 feet and eight inches across and 86 feet high—one foot for each year of the century to the date of its design in 1886. At the time of construction, the building had water, but no electricity, central heating, or indoor plumbing.

In 1938, in order to "modernize" the building, the exterior was stripped of all the ornamental detail, including the cupola, two blind Justices, and two American Eagles. In the interior, the ceilings were lowered and the north stairway removed.

During 1991 to 1993, the building was restored to its original form with the assistance of architects Cardwell/Thomas Associates.

The exterior restoration included restoration of the cupola and replicas of the American Eagles and Justices. The interior restoration, including the north interior stairway and, more importantly, the restoration of the courtroom to its original configuration, features the only courtroom in the state with balconies for spectators. All the other features are also originals.

The building's other features include delicate features on its pediment, steel steps in front and back made at the Walla Walla Foundry, and the jail in the basement taken from the brig of a ship. On the lawn in front of the building are two bronze Civil War cannons, which were obtained from the United States War Department in 1915.

This courthouse was listed in the National Registry of Historic Places in 1975.

The balcony behind the jury box in the courtroom.

The Cowlitz County Courthouse, now used for administration purposes (1923).

C o w l i t z   C o u n t y

Cowlitz County was created by the first Washington territorial legislature in 1854. The county was named after the Indians who lived along the Cowlitz River. The first county seat was established in 1854 at Montecello, a town later swept away by flood in 1867. Before that flood, however, the county seat had been moved to Freeport in 1865. In the 1872 election, the voters again moved the county seat to Kalama, where it remained through a number of hotly contested elections. Finally, in 1922, the county seat was moved to Kelso, where it remains today.

The first courthouse built for that purpose was constructed in 1923. Although the courts and other related functions have been moved to a new courthouse, the 1923 structure is still in use for county administration.

The 1923 courthouse was designed by architect W. W. Lucius of Portland, Oregon, and constructed by contractor C. F. Martin at a cost of $144,807, somewhat over budget. An addition was added to the courthouse using Works Progress Administration funds in 1939, changing its configuration to a rectangle. The addition was designed by architect Ray V. Weatherby and constructed by N. Torbit.

The building consists of three stories faced with red brick and based loosely on classical motifs, sometimes referred to as a Diluted Classical style. It has a heavy wooden pediment visually supported by concrete pilasters with ornate capitals. Like many courthouses constructed in the 1920s, the building has multiple-pane, wood-framed windows.

The original entrance faces south onto Academy Street from where it is approached by numerous wide stairs.

The present-day Douglas County Courthouse (1905).

D o u g l a s   C o u n t y

ouglas County was originally part of Lincoln County, but was separated from it in 1883. It was named after Steven A. Douglas, a former chairman of the United States Commission of Territories. Originally, the county included a town called Okanogan, near Douglas, which was designated as the temporary county seat. In 1886, voters elected Waterville as the county seat, where it remains today.

The present brick and stone courthouse was completed in 1907 at a cost of $32,000. The earlier courthouse was destroyed by fire. The courthouse was designed by architect Newton C. Gaunt of Portland, Oregon, who had previously designed the Wahkiakum County Courthouse at Cathlamet. The building contractor was William Oliver. The courthouse was designed in the California, or Spanish, Mission style of architecture. Another description of the architecture has it in the Richardsonian style with a Queen Anne cupola. The courthouse has recently been restored.

While the geography of the land seems appropriate to the style, the actual dimensions of the building do not appear in keeping with it. An interesting feature of the original design and construction was the inside glass dome over the courtroom designed to provide lighting. While the dome still exists, a false ceiling has been installed in the courtroom, which is now illuminated by electricity.

This courthouse was the first of three to be constructed in the Mission style, the other two being the Okanogan and Snohomish County courthouses.

A close-up of the courthouse tower, or cupola.

33

Ferry County Courthouse, circa 1908, courtesy of the Ferry County Historical Society.

F e r r y   C o u n t y

Ferry County was organized in 1899, 10 years after Washington became a state. It was formed from a portion of Stevens County and was named after Elisha P. Ferry, Washington's first governor. The county includes the Colville Indian Reservation. The county seat is in the town of Republic, which was once known as Eureka Gold Mining Camp.

By 1900, Republic was the center of a booming mining area, and the population was undoubtedly more than what it is today.

The original county courthouse was the frame building pictured here. It was destroyed by fire in 1935. After the fire, county business was conducted in the Republic City Hall until a new modern courthouse was completed in 1936.

F r a n k l i n   C o u n t y

Franklin County, named after Benjamin Franklin, was carved out of Whitman County in 1883. The first county seat was in the town of Ainsworth, but that was changed to Pasco by the 1885 election.

The present two-story brick courthouse was completed and dedicated in early 1913. The architect was C. Lewis Wilson & Co., listed as being from Seattle. Earlier, in 1910, the same architectural firm designed the Pacific County Courthouse in South Bend, but they were listed as being from Chehalis at that time. Apparently, the publicity received from the design of the Pacific County Courthouse (labeled the "Gilded Palace of Extravagance") was sufficient to increase their business and perhaps enable the firm to move to the larger city.

Some elaborate woodwork in the courthouse interior.

The style of the architecture is a Neo-Classic style similar to the earlier one at South Bend. Inside the courthouse, we find the use of art glass in the dome and the names of the towns existing in the county in 1912 around the dome in a different-colored glass. Below the dome and above each office entry is a large F, which is also found in the middle of the lower tile floor, signifying the first initial of the county. Other interesting features include the clock in the building lobby, the wall panels, mosaic tile floors, marble stairs, and scagliola wall and column finishes.

The original courtroom remains in use to-day. The large safe for valuable records built by Mosler Safe Co. also remains. The courthouse was entered in the National Registry of Historic Buildings in 1978.

The present Franklin County Courthouse (1912).

The intricate mosaic design of the lobby floor.

Franklin County
(c o n t i n u e d)

Interesting features of the cupola are in the covering of sheet metal rather than the copper called for by the architect and the existence of dormers for clocks that were never installed. Consideration is being given to implementing both of these. The exterior of this building is of brick and limestone. The building was constructed by Misho & Grant at a cost of $82,016. There is no record of the builders' home base.

In 1971, a Public Safety Building was added to the rear of the courthouse. In 1974 the courthouse suffered some damage when a packaged bomb sent to judge James Lawless exploded in his chambers. In 1976, the original courthouse was rehabilitated at a cost of approximately $700,000.

The art glass dome.

Garfield County

Garfield County was created in 1881 out of a portion of Columbia County and named after President James A. Garfield, whose portrait hangs in its courthouse.

Upon the county's creation, Pataka Creek (later Pataka City) was designated the temporary county seat. In 1882, a bitter fight took place between Pomeroy and Pataka City to determine the location of the permanent county seat. While Pomeroy won the election, a controversy ensued that had to be settled by the United States Congress in 1884. It is the only county seat in Washington to have been designated by Congress.

In 1901, after a fire destroyed most of the town, the present courthouse was constructed. The architect of this courthouse was Charles Burggraph of Albany, Oregon. The builder was Spokane contractor, August Ilse, and the cost of the construction was $19,583.

The specifications for the building called for the face brick to be cherry red in color and well burned and hard, but it seems someone fudged on the brick, as the exterior brick of the courthouse had to be painted three years later.

This Victorian-era courthouse with Queen Anne features has a Lady Justice with her scales on the roof and a statue of Governor Samuel Cosgrove on the lawn. He was the only governor to come from Pomeroy County. There is a clock in a dormer below Lady Justice operated by a small electric motor.

Considerable restoration of the courthouse has taken place in the interior, and the original courtroom has been restored, including the original seats of oak with wire hat racks for men's hats under each seat.

In the county auditor's office, there is an unusual wall clock that was installed in 1919. The clock, made by the Standard Time Co. of Springfield, Massachusetts, operates by a combination of electricity and a long pendulum.

The courthouse was entered in the National Registry of Historic Places in 1977.

The present-day Garfield County Courthouse (1901).

A courtroom seat with wire men's hat rack beneath.

Garfield County
(c o n t i n u e d)

The auditor's clock.

The courtroom with restored furnishings.

The present-day Grant County Courthouse (1917).

Grant County was one of the last counties to be created in Washington. In 1909, the legislature divided Douglas County into two parts, one of which was named in honor of Ulysses S. Grant. The other part retained the name of Douglas. Ephrata was immediately determined to be the county seat of newly formed Grant County.

The first courthouse was built in 1909 at a cost of $4,795. It is no longer in use as a public facility, but serves as the home of the Community Methodist Church.

The present courthouse was constructed in 1917. It was designed in the Neo-Classical Revival style by architect George H. Keith of Spokane, who had earlier designed the Okanogan County Courthouse. Portions of the county building, including the original ourthouse, are served by a geothermal heating system utilizing water from a nearby hot spring.

The courthouse is registered in the National Registry of Historic Places.

The courthouse cornerstone.   *A close-up of the front columns.*

Grays Harbor County

Grays Harbor County was established in 1854 as Chehalis County and named after the Native American tribe of the same name. "Chehalis" is a Native American word said to mean "sand." The first county seat was actually in Pacific County at Bruceport on Willapa Bay. It was not until 1860 that a legislative act put the county seat near Montesano. Although subsequent attempts were made by Aberdeen and Hoquiam to lure the county seat away, and even to split the county, it remains to this day at Montesano. The county name was ultimately changed to Grays Harbor, after Captain Robert Gray, who discovered the harbor in 1792.

Behind judge's bench.

Lobby mural.

The present-day Grays Harbor County Courthouse (1911).

Interior mural.

Interior dome.

Grays Harbor County
(c o n t i n u e d)

The present courthouse at Montesano was completed in 1911. It was designed by architect Watson Vernon of Aberdeen, Washington, and the main building was constructed by Syelliason & Sando of Seattle at an approximate total cost of $193,470. The architect's fees were five percent of that total. The design of the courthouse is in the Beaux Arts Roman Revival style.

The courthouse has many outstanding and unique features. Its exterior walls are of Tenino sandstone, and the roof was of copper (now replaced with steel). The building consists of three stories and a two-story clock tower containing a clock made by E. Howard and Company of Boston, Massachusetts. This is undoubtedly the same company elsewhere reported as E. Howard Tower Clock Co. and E. Howard Watch & Clock Company. This large clock, with dials measuring seven feet, two inches in diameter and numerals 14 feet high, was originally operated by weights that gradually fell down a distance of 13 feet and three inches to move the hands in unison through a universal joint system. They were then manually rewound with a hard crank. Later, a battery-operated motor was installed for the rewinding, and finally, an AC-DC motor was installed, which is used today.

Of great interest are the two murals in the main hall opposite each other as well as those in the courtroom. The murals were done by two well-known artists. One mural in the hall depicting Captain Robert Gray's landing in 1792 was done on canvas by Franz Biberstein, a Swiss-born artist from Milwaukee, Wisconsin. The opposite mural was done by Franz Rohrbeck, a German-born artist who also painted murals for the Brown County Courthouse in Green Bay, Wisconsin. Rohrbeck's mural depicts a historic treaty with Native Americans concluded at Cosmopolis, Washington, in 1855. In the painting, Territorial Governor Isaac Stevens stands facing the chiefs. It is interesting to observe that the dress of the Native Americans in both murals is not the dress of the area, but rather of the Plains tribes.

In the cupola below the clock tower is a section of art-stained glass, which, with the exception of a few pieces, remains as constructed. Some of the original light fixtures are also still in place.

The courthouse suffered severe damage in the 1999 earthquake centered at nearby Satsop and has now undergone a major renovation.

Scenes from dome.

The 1890 Island County Courthouse, courtesy of the Island County Historical Society.

I s l a n d   C o u n t y

Island County was created in 1853. Initially, it contained Whidbey and Camano islands and the area later to become Snohomish,   Skagit, Whatcom, and San Juan counties.

The first county seat was at Coveland, where the first courthouse, a wooden structure, was constructed in 1855. That courthouse included a store.

The first building to be constructed for use solely as a courthouse was built in Coupeville on Whidbey Island in 1890. It was torn down when the new courthouse in Coupeville was dedicated in 1949. Pictured here is the 1890 courthouse.

J e f f e r s o n　　　C o u n t y

Jefferson County was created in 1852 out of Thurston County while Washington was still a territory of the United States. It stretched from Puget Sound to the Pacific Ocean and included what is now Clallam County. Port Townsend, which had been named after the Marquis of Townshend in 1792 by Captain Vancouver, became the county seat.

One of the earlier courthouses, known as the Fowler Building and built in 1874, still stands and is occupied today.

Construction of the present courthouse was begun in 1890 shortly after Washington became a state in 1889.

The courthouse is high on a hill overlooking the city of Port Townsend and Admiralty Inlet. Seattle architect Willis A. Ritchie designed it, and the style had been characterized as Romanesque, but is sometimes referred to by others as a combination of Romanesque and Gothic architecture or as a variation on Medieval Chateau. Ritchie was also the architect of other county courthouses in Washington and the designer of numerous other buildings in Seattle when the Central District was being rebuilt after the fire of 1889.

Front view depicting stonework.

The building was constructed by John Rigby, a contractor, at a cost of between $125,000 and $150,000. The building itself sits on huge granite boulders, and its walls are of brick. The exterior brick is a deep red, high-quality brick, shipped from St. Louis, Missouri.

The present-day Jefferson County Courthouse (1891).

Carved wooden panel in the courtroom.

Jefferson County
(c o n t i n u e d)

The interior brick is a softer, low-quality local brick. The lower part of the building is faced with sandstone brought down from Alaska. The lower portion of the corridor walls is covered with a dark wainscoting, and the floors in the main halls are of geometrically patterned quarry tile. The second-floor courtroom has some intricately carved oak panels.

Most conspicuous is the huge clock tower rising 124 feet above the building with solid columns on each corner. The tower houses a unique clockworks with four faces and a bell that rings every hour. Both were built of solid brass by E. Howard Watch & Clock Company of Boston, Massachusetts, in 1890. While a few of the clock parts have been replaced and the clock refurbished, it still functions today. The bell has received a new hammer and also continues to function.

This magnificent courthouse may require some major construction in the years to come if it is to be preserved.

This courthouse is in the National Registry of Historic Places.

Old bookcase in the law library.

Courtroom.

King County Courthouse (1891) Courtesy of MSCUA, University of Washington Libraries; photo by A. Curtis, No. 915.

K i n g C o u n t y

King County was created in 1852 and originally encompassed the area that later became Mason and Kitsap counties. The county was named after William King, the thirteenth vice president of the United States. Seattle, named after Indian chief Sealth, was chosen as the county seat.

King County's first courthouse was built in 1882 and was used until 1891, when it was sold to Seattle to be used as a city hall. It became known as the "Katzenjammer Castle" because of all the additions added to it.

In 1891, a new courthouse designed by architect Willis A. Ritchie was completed. Ritchie had only recently arrived from Kansas, and this and the Jefferson County Courthouse were among his first major projects. The courthouse had to be reached from the business district by a steep ascent and, therefore, to the lawyers it became known as the courthouse on "Profanity Hill." This courthouse was torn down after a new county-city building was completed in 1916. The new building was designed by Seattle architect A.W. Gould. In the 1920s, five additional stories were added, thus changing its appearance. In the early 1960s, the city of Seattle moved out and it became the King County Courthouse.

King County Courthouse prior to additions (1916) Courtesy of MSCUA, University of Washington Libraries; photo by C.F. Todd, No. 12353.

The 1892 Kitsap County Courthouse, courtesy of the Kitsap County Historical Society Museum, Ward Collection, No.88-15.

K i t s a p   C o u n t y

Kitsap County was created in 1857 out of a portion of King and Jefferson counties. The original name given the county was "Slaughter" after a lieutenant who had been killed by Indians. A short time later, the name was changed to "Kitsap" after a well-known Indian chief of the time whose name meant "brave."

The county seat was located in Port Madison by the election of 1861 and it remained there for 31 years. Twice in the years after 1861, an election designated Teekalet to be the new county seat, but the county records were never moved there.

In 1891, another election was had, and Sydney was designated the new county seat. The post office name for Sydney was Port Orchard and when the post office refused to change the name, the legislature changed the name of Sydney to fit the post office.

In 1892, a courthouse was built in Port Orchard. It was remodeled in 1914 and finally torn down in 1932 and replaced by a new courthouse. The 1932 courthouse remains, but a new Kitsap County Administration Building constructed in 1949 is located in front of it. Pictured here is the 1914 courthouse.

The 1904 Kittitas County Courthouse, courtesy of the Kittitas County Historical Society.

Kittitas County

K ittitas County was created in 1883 from a part of Yakima County. Subsequently, in 1899, a portion of the county was taken away to create Chelan County.

"Kittitas" is a Native American word that has two possible interpretations. It is said to mean either "plenty food" or "gray gravel bank." Either could apply, since the Yakima River runs through a lush valley in the county.

Ellensburg has always been the county seat. John Shoudy, who came to the area in the early 1870s and established the central business district, named the town after his wife, Ellen.

The first courthouse in the county was a two-story brick building constructed in 1904. It was replaced in 1955 by the presently occupied low modern building. The 1904 courthouse is pictured here.

The 1889 Klickitat County Courthouse, courtesy of the Klickitat County Historical Society archives.

Klickitat County

T his county was created in 1859 along the north shore of the Columbia River. The county was named after the Native American tribe who inhabited the area—the Clickitat.

The first county seat was at Rockland Flats where Dallesport is today. There, the commissioners rented a shack as a courthouse. In 1879, the county populace voted to change the county seat to Goldendale, where it remains.

In 1889, the two-story brick courthouse pictured here was constructed. Although the cupola was removed in later years, this building remained in use as the courthouse until 1941, when a new modern courthouse was constructed. When that was completed, the old courthouse was destroyed.

L e w i s   C o u n t y

Lewis County was originally part of the Vancouver District of the Oregon Territory. In 1845, the districts were changed to counties and the Vancouver District was divided. Lewis County was created out of all the land north of the Columbia River to 54° 40' and west of the Cowlitz River to the Pacific Ocean. Like its counterpart from the Vancouver District, Clark County, it was named after the other leader of the Lewis and Clark Expedition, Meriwether Lewis.

The earliest county seat and courthouse were at Mary's Corner on Jackson Prairie a few miles south of Chehalis. In 1862, the legislature moved the county seat to Claquato, a couple miles west of Chehalis. When it appeared the railroad wasn't going through Claquato, the town began its decline, and in 1872, the county seat was moved to Chehalis, then known as Saundersville. At that time, the town name was changed to "Chehalis," which was the Native American name given to the nearby river.

The first courthouse was built in 1874, with the upper story used as a schoolhouse. The Chehalis Library became the courthouse in 1901 and remained in use until 1927, when the present-day courthouse was completed.

The architect of the courthouse was J. deForest Griffin of Chehalis. The first unit (foundation and concrete shell) was constructed by S. Christian Erickson of Tacoma, Washington, who had formerly been a Chehalis resident. The building was completed by Portland, Oregon, contractor, Settergren Bros. Reports of the building's cost varied, but the newspaper of the day reported it at $420,000.

The present-day Lewis County Courthouse (1927).

Interior view to staircase.

Lewis County
(c o n t i n u e d)

The courthouse has a number of interesting features. The parapet is exaggerated into an attic story, but without openings. The face of it is decorated with portrait busts in bas-relief of Meriwether Lewis and George Washington, for whom the county and state were named. On the north side between the two busts is the following inscription in Roman letters:

COURTHOUSE OF THE COUNTY OF LEWIS ERECTED
BY THE PEOPLE AND DEDICATED TO THE
ADVANCEMENT OF JUSTICE

On the Main Street-side of the building is a quote from George Washington:

LET US RAISE A STANDARD
TO WHICH THE WISE AND HONEST
CAN REPAIR

The architectural-cut cast stone in various colors and textures sent down from Seattle was used on the exterior of the courthouse. The exterior courthouse doors are of bronze.

Inside the courthouse corridor is a sculptured panel depicting Meriwether Lewis by James A. Wehn of Seattle, who also did the sculpture of Chief Sealth in that city. Elsewhere in the interior is fine mahogany woodwork.

Sculptured panel of Meriwether Lewis.

The present-day Lincoln County Courthouse prior to modernization, courtesy of the Lincoln County Historical Society (1897).

L i n c o l n   C o u n t y

This county, named after Abraham Lincoln, was created in 1883 as the result of a division of Spokane County. Four days after its creation, it lost half of its area to newly created Douglas County.

While Davenport was named the temporary county seat, a contest ensued between Sprague, Harrington, and Davenport. Sprague won the vote count, but the election was more than suspect because Sprague received more votes than the entire population of the county. Nevertheless, Sprague was declared the winner and remained the county seat until an election in 1896, when it was moved to Davenport.

After the selection of Davenport, a new courthouse was constructed in 1897 and remains in use today. The architects for the new courthouse were Dow & Hubbell of Spokane, and the builder was a local man by the name of Fred Baske. The cost of the courthouse was $12,000.

The original courthouse was small, and in 1906, an addition was added to the rear, nearly doubling the original size. It was decided that the new addition gave the appearance of an imbalance of scale, however, and a new front entrance was added. One of the significant changes made was the realignment of the stairway inside, which originally looked ahead to a window giving light on the stairway.

In 1938, the building was somewhat modernized and new terrazzo floors were added.

A closer view of the courthouse entrance.

In 1995, a juvenile delinquent who had been the subject of discipline climbed the fire escape and set fire to the second-floor office of the juvenile authorities, thinking this would solve his problems. The result was a fire that destroyed the roof and second floor in a blaze that could be seen for miles.

By 1996, the building had been restored, more or less, to its original state. One change was the increase in elevation to accommodate a third-floor area.

The present-day Mason County Courthouse (1929).

The courthouse cornerstone.

DEDICATED
TO THE CITIZENS OF
MASON COUNTY
A·D·1929

Mason County was created by the first territorial legislature in 1854 out of a part of Thurston County and given the name of Sawamish County. The name was changed to Mason in 1864 to honor C.A. Mason, secretary to the territorial governor. The first county seat was at Oakland (then Mt. Olive), but was moved to Shelton in 1888, that town being named after its first mayor, David Shelton.

The present three-story courthouse was constructed in 1929. The courthouse was designed by architect Joseph H. Wohleb of Olympia, Washington, who later designed the Thurston County Courthouse. The builder was E. P. Brewster, who had bid $105,679 for the cost of construction.

The facing of the building is a four-inch layer of Tenino sandstone — a widely used stone at the time — and overlaps brick and concrete walls. The windows have terra cotta sills, and the same material covers the columns. Although it contains no unusual features, the original courtroom is still in use on the second floor.

The present-day Okanagan County Courthouse, prior to addition (1915).

Okanogan County

Okanogan County was formed in 1888 out of a part of Stevens County with the mining town of Ruby as its first county seat. That same year an election took place, and the county seat was moved to the town of Conconully.

In 1914, a new election took place with the towns of Omak, Riverside, and Okanogan all vying for the location. Okanogan won out. The name "Okanogan" is derived from the Native American word "ookenawkane," meaning "rendezvous."

After the 1914 election, the county commissioners immediately set to work planning a new courthouse. They engaged George H. Keith, a well-known Spokane architect, to design the building. The resulting design was a Spanish Mission style, sometimes referred to as Spanish Colonial Revival, similar to that of the earlier courthouse at Waterville in Douglas County and at Everett in Snohomish County.

Courthouse entrance.

The contract for construction was awarded to D.D. Davenport of Omak, Washington, for $30,000. The building was a three-story stucco building with a metal-simulated tile roof and hollow terra cotta walls.

The original courtroom on the second floor featured an inside glass dome for lighting. While the courtroom itself remains essentially unchanged, a false ceiling and fluorescent lighting have been installed.

It appears that the tower was designed for a clock, but like some other courthouses, the clock was never installed.

The courthouse was originally constructed with canvas awnings over the windows to keep the rooms cooler during hot Eastern Washington summers.

In 1950, a new addition, designed by well-known Wenatchee architect Ludwig Solberg, was added at a cost of $225,000. It was dedicated by Governor Arthur B. Langlie.

The courthouse is registered in the National Registry of Historic Places.

P a c i f i c   C o u n t y

In 1851, Pacific County was one of the first counties to be created in Washington State. This was long before statehood, which did not come until 1889. The county was carved out of a portion of Lewis County and had its boundaries altered several times through 1879.

Pacific County had its share of struggles over the location of the county seat. Originally, it was located at Pacific City on Cape Disappointment, a community that no longer exists. The first court session, however, took place at Chinook, or Chinookville, as it was sometimes called. Ultimately, Oysterville became the county seat, and a courthouse was constructed there in 1876. In 1892, the Pacific County voters determined that the county seat should be moved to South Bend, where it remains to this day. After several struggles over the county records, they were finally housed in the new courthouse at South Bend.

The present courthouse was constructed in 1910 on "Quality Hill" overlooking South Bend's business district on U.S. Highway 101 and the south bend of the Willapa River. The courthouse was entered in the National Registry of Historic Places on July 20, 1977.

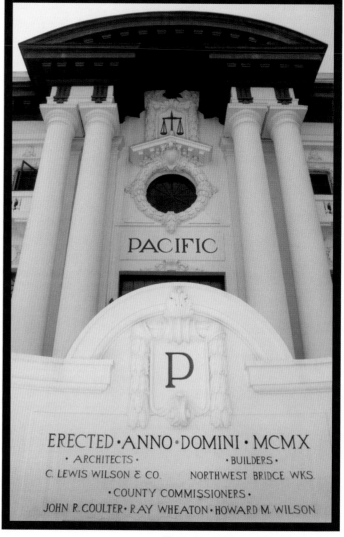

Front entrance to the courthouse.

The present-day Pacific County Courthouse (1910).

Pacific County
(c o n t i n u e d)

Interior mural.

Interior mural.

In the years following its construction, the local press referred to the courthouse as the "Gilded Palace of Extravagance." Indeed, it is quite unique and certainly would have been considered pretentious at the time of its construction in 1910. Among its exceptional features, many of which are pictured here, are the beautiful 29-foot art glass rotunda, the panel paintings, and the original courtroom with its lighting hood of art glass over the judge's desk.

The courthouse architect was C. Lewis Wilson & Co. of Chehalis, Washington, and the contractor responsible for the construction was Northwest Bridge Works of Portland, Oregon. The final cost of construction was $132,000. Various minor remodelings have taken place, and in 1980, the glasswork of the dome was restored to its original brilliance at a cost that exceeded the original construction cost for the whole building, glass and all.

The architectural style of the courthouse has been characterized as Classic Revival or Second Renaissance style.

*The courtroom with art glass overhead
and above the judge's desk.*

Art glass dome below the rotunda.

Dome light in courtroom.

77

The present-day Pend Oreille Courthouse (1915).

P e n d   O r e i l l e   C o u n t y

Pend Oreille County was formed in 1911 out of a portion of Stevens County. The temporary county seat at Newport became permanent as a result of the 1912 election. Newport was a well-established community at that time, as it was an important shipping point for steamers traveling the Pend Oreille River between the zinc and lead mines of the Metaline District and Newport.

In 1915, the county commissioners determined that the county should build its own courthouse. Architects throughout Washington and Idaho were invited to submit sketches of a proposed courthouse, which was to have a floor space of about 15,000 square feet and a cost not to exceed $27,000. Based on the sketches submitted, architects Williams & Williams of Coeur d'Alene, Idaho, were chosen to design a courthouse within the parameters noted.

After settling on the design, bids for the construction were requested. The lowest bid was offered by T.W. Hartness of Spokane, and he was awarded the contract for $19,648. A separate contract of $3,275 was awarded for the heating and plumbing. The site itself was donated. In December 1915, the building was completed at a total cost of $26,548, well within the budget, a fact noted by the *Spokesman-Review* of Spokane, which expressed its congratulations on that fact.

The building itself was built of buff-colored pressed brick facing and terra cotta trim.

Of note is the gray cornerstone of terrazzo. Inside the stone was placed a metal box containing news articles of the day about the creation of the county.

The 1893 Pierce County Courthouse, courtesy of the Tacoma Public Library, No. TPL 2532.

Pierce County

Pierce County was carved out of a portion of Thurston County in 1852. The new county was named for Franklin Pierce, the fourteenth President of the United States.

Steilacoom was the first county seat, and a courthouse was built there in 1853. That building served as the courthouse until 1880, when the county seat was moved to Tacoma. The name "Tacoma" is a Puyallup word that is said to mean "Big Mother of All," possibly referring to Mt. Rainier. By the 1880s, Tacoma was a world port and the terminus of the Northern Pacific Railroad's transcontinental line.

The first court records in Tacoma were deposited in several places until a courthouse was erected on Broadway in 1882. That courthouse served until 1893, when a new courthouse was erected.

Architects Proctor & Dennis designed the new courthouse in the Romanesque style, and contractor John T. Long of Wilkeson constructed it. It was built of Pittsburgh gray freestone and finished with Tenino bluestone. The courthouse was said to be patterned after the courthouse in Pittsburgh, Pennsylvania, and was designed by H. H. Richardson, a famous American architect. The Romanesque style of architecture was popular at the time. Willis A. Ritchie had already designed the courthouse in Port Townsend in the same style, and others of similar architecture were to follow.

The 230-foot tower on the courthouse was severely damaged during the earthquake in 1949. Ten years later, the old courthouse was demolished and replaced by a new modern county-city building.

The present-day San Juan County Courthouse (1906).

San Juan County

San Juan County is an archipelago consisting of 174 islands. It is the only county in the state not accessible by automobile. The county was established in 1873. At different times, it had been a part of the Vancouver District, Lewis County, Thurston County, Island County, and Whatcom County.

In 1873, Otis on Lopez Island and Friday Harbor on San Juan Island competed for the county seat designation. The election that year gave the title to Friday Harbor, where the county seat remains today.

San Juan Island is the site of the "Pig War" with Great Britain, which was finally resolved in 1872 by Kaiser Wilhelm I, who awarded the area to the United States.

A front view of the courthouse.

The present brick courthouse was built in 1906. An addition of dissimilar architecture has since been added.

The architect of the 1906 courthouse was W. P. White of Seattle, Washington, whose plans and specifications were accepted, and a payment of three percent of the cost of the construction was to be the fee. A proviso of the fee agreement was that the new courthouse had to be constructed at a cost of no more than $13,000. The design criteria for the new courthouse were that it be a fireproof building of suitable architectural design and with a fireproof vault.

Bids were called for, and John S. Shockey of Bellingham was the low bidder at $13,950 and was awarded the contract. The building was to be completed by October 15, 1906 or a penalty of $10 per day would be assessed for delayed completion. The commissioner then proceeded to authorize a bond issue for $14,000 to pay for the construction. That courthouse remains in use today.

The present-day Skagit County Courthouse (1924).

A front view of the courthouse with cannon.

I n 1883, Skagit County was formed from a part of Whatcom County. The word "Skagit" is a Native American word meaning "wildcat." Since most of the travel in those days was by boat, the first county seat was established at La Conner on the water across from Fidalgo Island, which had been settled first.

A series of frame buildings served as the first county courthouses, including a Grange Hall, which had also been used as the first federal courthouse north of Seattle. As Mount Vernon grew, pressure mounted to move the courthouse there, and in 1884, the voters approved a measure to move the county seat to Mount Vernon.

A courthouse now known as the Matheson Building was constructed a short time after the move. In 1924, a new courthouse, pictured here, was completed. The architect of the second courthouse was T. F. Doane, and it was constructed by A. D. Freis, a general contractor in the area.

The 1903 Skamania County Courthouse, courtesy of the Skamania County Historical Society, No. 1990:20.10.

Skamania County

Skamania County was formed in 1854 with the Columbia River as its southern boundary. The name "Skamania" is a Native American word meaning "swift water."

The population dropped significantly over the next few years, and in January 1865, Skamania County ceased to exist and its area was divided between Klickitat and Clark counties. The county was re-established in 1867.

The first county seat was at Cascades, a town near the Cascade Rapids. In 1893, the county seat was changed to Stevenson. It has been reported that this move took place because some citizens of Stevenson stole the county records and moved them there. Although legal action was threatened, the flood of 1894 made it obvious that the records would be safer in Stevenson after Cascades suffered severe damage from the flood.

A new courthouse was constructed and awaited the deposit of the stolen records. In 1903, the original courthouse, pictured here, was replaced with a two-story wooden structure, which served until 1949, when the present-day courthouse was constructed.

The present-day Snohomish County Courthouse (1911).

Snohomish County

Snohomish County was created in 1861. The first county seat was at Mukilteo. A short time later, still in 1861, the county seat was moved to Snohomish City. In 1898, after three court battles that reached the state's Supreme Court, the county seat was moved to Everett, where a new courthouse, constructed in 1897 in the Romanesque or Chateauesque style, awaited government. That courthouse had been designed by August F. Heinde.

A closer view of the courthouse tower.

In 1909, the 1897 courthouse was destroyed by an arson fire. In 1911, a new California Mission style courthouse was completed. This courthouse was designed by architects Siebrand and Heide of Seattle and built by the construction firm of Olson & Melt of Seattle on the foundation of the previous courthouse. Although newer buildings surround it, the Mission style courthouse remains in use for county government.

In the center of the building is a square clock tower rising a considerable height above the roofline. Above the clock area is a belfry, and on top of that is an octagonal drum and stucco dome painted gold.

The building, with its buff-colored stucco finish and red tiled roof, is typical of the Mission style. Undoubtedly, architect Heide was influenced by the Mission style buildings that were displayed at the Centennial Expedition in Portland, Oregon, in 1905, where Heide had designed the Washington State Building for the fair. The official buildings of the fair were described as a Free Renaissance of the Spanish type.

Although, by 1910, other buildings of this style were designed and built in the Seattle area, the Snohomish County Courthouse was the first major building of that style built west of the Cascades in a climate seemingly unsuited for the style. A similar style courthouse was to follow in Okanogan County in eastern Washington.

Spokane County

Spokane County was officially created from a portion of Walla Walla County in 1860. It was a huge county, extending to the Rocky Mountains on the east, north to the 49th parallel, south to the Snake River, and west to the Columbia River. However, in 1863, the territory of Idaho was created, thereby removing two-thirds of the county and setting the eastern boundary of Washington State. The following year, Spokane County became part of Stevens County. It was re-created from Stevens in 1879, and in 1883, Lincoln County was carved out of what remained of Spokane County, leaving it as it is today.

Spokane Falls was the first county seat, but an election was held in 1880 and Cheney became the county seat (reportedly having taken the records by theft). Finally, in 1886, Spokane became the permanent county seat. "Spokane" is a Native American word meaning "child of the sun."

When the time came for a larger and more permanent courthouse, the commissioners advertised a contest for the best design. The contest was won by Seattle architect Willis A. Ritchie, then 29 years old. He moved to Spokane permanently before this work was completed. He had already designed several other courthouses in Washington, one in the Romanesque style and another in a

Classical style. This time, however, his design was a replica of sixteenth-century French Renaissance and is said to resemble two famous sixteenth-century chateaux: Chateau du Chambord (1519) and Chateau d'Azay Le Rideau (1516), both in the Loire Valley of France.

A closer view of the main tower of present day Courthouse.

The present-day Spokane County Courthouse (1895).

A different perspective.

S p o k a n e   C o u n t y
(c o n t i n u e d)

The contract for construction was awarded, and construction began in 1893. The cost of the building was $273,600, a great sum in 1895, the year of its completion, but insignificant in terms of its latest valuation in excess of $22,000,000. In all probability, it could not be duplicated.

The building sits on a four-foot solid rock foundation. The roof was made of imported slate shingles. The brick, however, was a local product of the Washington Brick and Lime Manufacturing Company.

Completion was hampered by a number of events. At one point during construction, the county commissioners asked Ritchie to resign because of his dispute with the superintendent of construction. Ritchie refused and was ultimately cleared by the grand jury after an investigation.

After opening, there was further discord when it was discovered some of the courthouse employees were living and doing their cooking in the building.

There has been some remodeling over the years and new facilities have been added to the rear, but this courthouse remains one of the more spectacular buildings in Washington.

A close-up of the minor towers.

Exterior scrollwork.

93

The 1898 Stevens County Courthouse, courtesy of the Stevens County Historical Society (Colville, WA).

S t e v e n s   C o u n t y

S tevens County was created in 1863 from a part of Walla Walla County. At the time of its creation, the county encompassed a vast area, including what is now Douglas, Ferry, Okanogan, Pend Oreille, and part of Chelan counties. Even the area to become Spokane County was later added. The county is named for the first territorial governor, Isaac Stevens. Although Pickney City was first chosen as the county seat, Colville became the final choice in 1883.

In 1898, a group of Colville citizens started a fund to build a new courthouse. They collected $5,000 and constructed most of the building before the county government took over to complete it. This courthouse, pictured here, remained in use for 41 years, until 1938, when a new courthouse was constructed.

The 1930 Thurston County Courthouse.

Thurston County was created in 1852. It was named after the first delegate to Congress from the Oregon Territory, Samuel R. Thurston. Included in its boundaries was the first settlement north of the Columbia River, Tumwater. Olympia, originally named Smithfield, became the county seat.

The entrance doors to the 1930 courthouse.

Until 1891, a series of temporary locations served as the courthouse. In 1891, a new courthouse construction commenced and was completed in 1892. This courthouse was designed by Willis A. Ritchie of Seattle, the designer of several other courthouses. That courthouse, constructed of Chuckanut stone from quarries in Whatcom County, still stands facing Sylvester Park. It was later sold to the state and from 1905 to 1927 it served as the state capitol building. The large clock tower on this building was destroyed by fire in 1928.

After the sale of the "Old State Capitol Building," a new courthouse was constructed, but it was torn down in 1930 and another courthouse was constructed across from the state capitol grounds. This courthouse still stands today, but is no longer used as a courthouse. It was designed by Joseph Wohleb, architect of the Mason County Courthouse. It has been replaced as a courthouse by a series of low modern buildings at a different location.

The present-day Wahkiakum County Courthouse (1923).

Wahkiakum County

Wahkiakum County was formed in 1854 and bears the name of a local tribe of Native Americans.

The first courthouse, a one-story wooden building, was built in Cathlamet in 1872. Despite efforts of the citizens of the town of Skamokawa, the county seat remained in Cathlamet. In 1891, a larger wooden building was constructed and an addition was built in 1900. This building remained the courthouse until 1921, when it was totally destroyed by fire.

The county commissioners then engaged a Portland, Oregon, architect, Newton C. Gauntt, to draw plans for a new fireproof courthouse. This new courthouse was then constructed by C. F. Martin, a general contractor, who was also building the Cowlitz County Courthouse, and was probably completed in 1923 at a cost of $36,513.13.

The courthouse is a three-story structure with a truncated hipped roof and outer walls of concrete covered with stucco. A large pediment appears in front of the roofline over the main entrance and is supported by two large columns on either side of the main entrance.

In 1994, extensive interior remodeling took place, upgrading the electrical and mechanical systems, installing appropriate cabling for computers, and a myriad of other much-needed upgrades.

The original floor plans placed the one superior courtroom at the rear of the second floor, but it has since been moved to the first floor. The courtroom is now a modern facility. The court is presided over by one judge serving both Wahkiakum and Pacific counties.

The courthouse itself is located on Cathlamet's main street, which is State Highway 4. The town's business district is clustered around a two-block area near the courthouse. While there are no particularly unique features to this courthouse, nevertheless, standing as it does on the main street of this small town, it is impressive.

The present-day Walla Walla County Courthouse (1915).

Walla Walla County

Walla Walla County was created in 1854 out of a part of Skamania County. Originally, and until the creation of Columbia County in 1875, it stretched eastward to the summit of the Rocky Mountains and included 70 million acres. The word "Walla Walla" is said to come from a Native American word meaning "Many Waters."

The present-day courthouse was built in 1915 at a total cost of $154,544.90, including the heating plant and walkways. The architectural style is Grecian with Doric columns. The architects were Osterman and Subert.

Alongside, and quite in contrast to the courthouse, sits the county jail, built in 1906 of red brick rather than the gray stone of the courthouse. Above the front entrance to the courthouse, there is the inscription:

JUDGE THYSELF WITH SINCERITY
AND THOU WILL JUDGE OTHERS
WITH CHARITY

Some of the more interesting interior features include the wooden banisters and the stone floor.

The Walla Walla County jail (1906).

The 1891 Whatcom County Courthouse, courtesy of the E.A. Heeb Collection, Whatcom Museum of History and Art, Bellingham, WA. No. 7377.

W h a t c o m   C o u n t y

Whatcom County was established by the territorial legislature in 1854. When first established, it also included what is now San Juan and Skagit counties. In 1873, the San Juan County area was taken away, and in 1883, the Skagit County area was also severed. The county seat has always been in the Bellingham area. The word "Whatcom" is a Native American word that has been interpreted by some to mean "rushing waters" and by others as meaning "noisy waters."

Several different buildings in the Bellingham area were used as the county courthouse until 1889, when construction of a new courthouse, built of Chuckanut stone, was begun and completed in 1891. This stone is native to the area and was widely used in building construction. The architect of this courthouse was Willis A. Ritchie, then of Seattle. He was, at the same time, designing the King County Courthouse.

In 1950, the 1889 courthouse was torn down, and a new concrete structure replaced it.

The 1890 Whitman County Courthouse, courtesy of the Historical Photograph Collections, Washington State University, No. 78346; photographer was Smilen Norde.

W h i t m a n   C o u n t y

Whitman County was carved out of Stevens County in 1871. It was named in honor of Marcus Whitman, a Walla Walla missionary. The area has always been known as the "Palouse Country," meaning "grassy hills" country, a word taken from the Palouse tribe of Native Americans who had inhabited the area. The county seat has always been in Colfax. However, Colfax was known as Belleville when first established.

The first courthouse was constructed during 1889-1890 in a stately Colonial style. It had the dubious distinction of having two men lynched out of one of its front windows in 1894. The old courthouse was torn down and a new one built on the same site in 1955.

The 1907 Yakima County Courthouse, courtesy of the Yakima Valley Museum.

Yakima County

Yakima County was formed in 1865. It was named after the Eyakima tribe of Native Americans. The name means "well-fed people."

As was typical in the early days, the county seat moved from location to location until it was finally established in Yakima City in 1870 as the result of an election. Yakima City was the town now known as Union Gap. The first courthouse and second courthouse were both constructed there. The second courthouse burned, as did all the records, in 1882.

The Northern Pacific Railroad came to the area in 1885 and moved the town and the courthouse four miles north to North Yakima. That courthouse also burned down in 1906.

The fourth courthouse was built in 1906 on the same location. The construction was of dark stone, above which was a facing of light brick. It had the usual tower of the period with a clock. This grand old courthouse was torn down in 1963 to make room for a new modern structure.

Appendix: Courthouse Architects

Architect	Courthouse Designed	Year Completed
Burggraph, Charles Albany, Oregon	Garfield	1901
Burrows, William Dayton, Washington	Columbia	1887
Doane, T. F. Address unknown	Skagit	1924
Dow & Hubbell Spokane, Washington	Lincoln	1897
Gaunt, Newton C. Portland, Oregon	Wahkiakum Douglas	1923 1924
Grant, Francis W. Seattle, Washington	Clallam	1915
Griffin J. deForest Chehalis, Washington	Lewis	1927
Heide, August F. Seattle, Washington	Snohomish	1911
Keith, George H. Spokane, Washington	Okanogan Grant	1915 1917

108

Architect	Courthouse Designed	Year Completed
Lucius, W. W. Portland, Oregon	Cowlitz	1923
Osterman & Subert Address unknown	Walla Walla	1915
Rasque, George W. Address unknown	Benton	1927
Ritchie, Willis A. Seattle/Spokane, Washington	Thurston Jefferson Spokane	1892 1892 1895
Solberg, Ludwig Address unknown	Chelan	1924
Vernon, Watson Aberdeen, Washington	Grays Harbor	1911
White, W. P. Seattle, Washington	San Juan	1906
Williams & Williams Coeur d'Alene, Idaho	Pend Oreille	1915
Wilson, C. Lewis Seattle, Washington	Pacific Franklin	1910 1912
Wohleb, Joseph H. Olympia, Washington	Mason Thurston	1929 1930

Glossary of Architecture and Building Terms

Art glass	generally refers to stained glass with designs
Bas-relief	projection of figures or forms from a flat background
Beaux Arts	in the Classical form of architectural style, Beaux Arts is characterized by grandiose compositions with a lot of detail and frequently characterized by colossal columns, often in pairs
Chateau	a style of architecture that is massive and irregular in form and silhouette and has steep, pitched roofs
California Mission	an architectural style characterized by simple arches, stuccoed exterior walls, and red tile roofs; the larger buildings usually have towers; sometimes referred to as Spanish Mission
Cupola	a small dome on either a circular or polygonal base and crowning the roof
Doric	one mode of an Order that is a column with a base, shaft, and capital; it may be Greek or Roman in origin
Dormer	most often, a window placed vertically in a sloping roof and usually installed to provide sleeping quarters
Finial	usually a detachable ornament on top of a gable or roof
Geothermal	the earth's internal heat
Hipped	a roof angle formed by the meeting of two sloping surfaces
Italianate	a style of architecture characterized by a rectangular (or square) building, usually topped with a cupola
Neo-Classic	an architectural style based on the Greek Order; there will frequently be large pedimented porticos flanked by large pilasters; also known as Neo-Classicism
Palladian	a Roman style of architecture derived from the works of Palladio; the Palladian motif generally consists of arches supported on minor columns and framed between larger engaged columns
Parapet	a low wall, usually on top of a building where there is a sudden drop
Pediment	a low, pitched gable above a portico
Pilaster	a pier, or rectangular column jutting slightly out from a wall
Queen Anne	a style of architecture characterized by a variety of forms and decorations; its architectural parts may include towers, turrets, bays, and more
Romanesque	an architectural style characterized by monochromatic stone or brick surfaces and semicircular arches for doors and windows; there are variations reflected in the Victorian variance and those used by H.H. Richardson, called Richardsonian Romanesque
Rotunda	generally, a room that is circular and domed, like the Pantheon
Scagliola	a manmade material resembling marble
Terra cotta	fired but unglazed clay used in wall coverings and ornamentation
Terrazzo	a floor finishing made of marble chips and cement mortar, ground and polished
Truncate	cut off to shorten; designed to make an abrupt termination

Bibliography

Biographical Dictionary of American Architects. *Los Angeles, CA: New Age Publishing, 1956.*

Blumenson, John J. G. *Identifying American Architecture, 2nd Edition.* New York: W. W. Norton & Company, Inc., 1981.

Hushagen, Richard. *Counties of the State of Washington,* 1986.

Jones, Sylvia Case and Myra Frederickson Casady. *From Cabin to Cupola.* Seattle, WA: Shorey Book Store, 1971.

Journal of Everett and Snohomish County History, *Number 5, Winter 1983.*

Kalez, Jay J. *"This town of ours...Spokane."* Spokane, WA: Lawton Printing, Inc., 1973.

Ochsner, Jeffrey Karl. *Shaping Seattle Architecture,* Seattle, WA: University of Washington Press, 1994.

Roberts, George and Jan Roberts. *Discover Historic Washington State.* Baldwin Park, CA: Gem Guides Book Company, 1999.

Stinson, William. *A View of the Falls, An Illustrated History of Spokane.* Windsor Publications, 1946.

Thorndike, Joseph J. *Three Centuries of Notable American Architects.* New York: American Heritage Publishing Co., Inc., 1981.

Turner, L. Roger and Marv Balousek. *Wisconsin's Historic Courthouses.* Oregon, WI: Badger Books, Inc., 1998.

Watkin, David. *A History of American Architecture.* New York: Thames & Hudson, Inc., 1986.

Woodbridge, Sally B. and Roger Montgomery. *Guide to Architecture in Washington State,* 1980.

Works Progress Administration. *Collection of County Histories.* Washington State Historical Society.